DOTS

D1297859

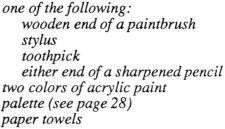

YOU WILL NEED:

one of the following:
    wooden end of a paintbrush
    stylus
    toothpick
    either end of a sharpened pencil
two colors of acrylic paint
palette (see page 28)
paper towels

For production work there are dot tools available that have dots formed in many shapes--flower, triangle, etc.

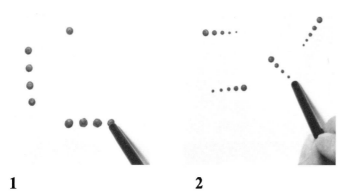

1   Dip the end of your brush or other tool in a nickel-size puddle of acrylic paint. Touch the tool to your paper. Presto! A perfect dot. Repeat dipping and touching to make dots of identical size.

2   To make a line of descending dots: do not re-load the tool after making the first dot. Rather, continue making dots and they will become progressively smaller. Generally, five dots is the most you can make in this manner.

1   **2**

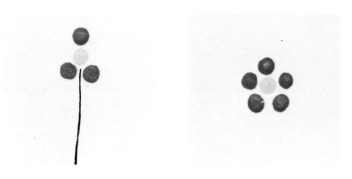

3   To make a five petal flower: begin with the center dot using one color, wipe tool clean. Make a dot directly above the center dot using the other color. Draw an imaginary line as shown. Reload the tool for each dot. Make a dot on each side of the imaginary line.

4   Make the final two dots as shown.

3   **4**

STITCHES & LIFELINE

YOU WILL NEED:

#00 liner brush
one color of acrylic paint
fine tip felt pen with permanent black
*   ink*
palette
paper towels
small bar of soap
tracing paper

To load a liner brush: put the tip of the brush in paint. While rolling the brush handle in your fingers, pull the brush tip toward you. This will give you a fine point to begin your stroke.

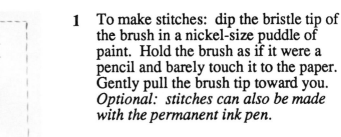

1

2

1 To make stitches: dip the bristle tip of the brush in a nickel-size puddle of paint. Hold the brush as if it were a pencil and barely touch it to the paper. Gently pull the brush tip toward you. *Optional: stitches can also be made with the permanent ink pen.*

2 Here are some different stitch patterns using a variety of stitch lengths.

3

4

3 To make the lifeline: dip the bristle tip of the brush in a nickel-size puddle of paint. Hold the brush as if it were a pencil and touch the point to the paper. Push it gently away from you then pull it down laying the brush on its side. This makes a "rick-rack" type motion that is thin on one side and thick on the other. It will take a little practice to make the lifeline flow smoothly.

4 Shown here are some different lifeline patterns using several line lengths.

BASIC STROKES
(also called daisy strokes or teardrops)

YOU WILL NEED:

#6 medium flat brush
#00 liner brush (to make smaller
strokes)
two colors of acrylic paint
palette
paper towels
small bar of soap
tracing paper

It will take a little practice to get these strokes exactly as you see here. Just take your time and practice on tracing paper. The fun begins soon!

1 To load your flat brush: put the tip of the brush in paint. Place the brush on a clean area of the palette. Take a stroke using first one side of the brush then the other side. Repeat making the stroke 2-4 times. This action will evenly blend the paint through the brush.

2 Load your flat brush with paint. Keep the tip at a 45° angle and touch the brush to the paper. The left corner of the brush should be higher than the right. Apply pressure as you slightly curve the brush to the left. Pull the brush toward you and <u>slowly</u> lift up making a pointed tail.

3 This basic stroke is made like the first one, just place the brush so the right corner is higher than the left. And curve the stroke to the right.

4 Hold your brush exactly as you did in step 3 but apply pressure and pull the brush straight toward you. As you begin to lift the brush, give it a 1/4 turn to the left. This will make the stroke end with a straight pointed tail.

1

2

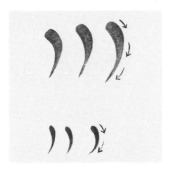

3

4

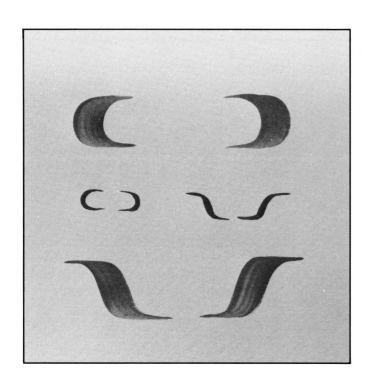

YOU WILL NEED:

#6 flat brush
#00 liner brush (to make smaller
*   strokes)*
palette
one color of acrylic paint
paper towel
small bar of soap

To load your flat brush follow step 1 on page 3.

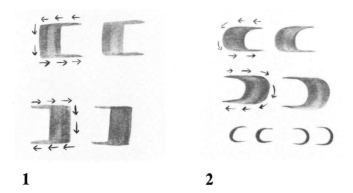

1 To make a "C": begin by making square "C's." Load your flat brush. Hold the brush straight up and as it barely touches the paper, slide it to your left. Then pull straight down using the full width of the brush. Now hold the brush straight up and as it barely touches the paper, slide it to your right. *Note: do not lift the brush as you make this stroke. Be sure to keep the legs of the "C" the same length and width.*

2 Make the "C" stroke again but round off the corners.

1   **2**

3 To make an "S": begin by making square "S's." Load your flat brush. Hold it straight up and as the brush barely touches the paper, slide it to your right. Then pull straight down using the full width of the brush. Now hold the brush straight up and as it barely touches the paper, slide it to your right. *Note: do not lift the brush as you make this stroke. Be sure to keep the legs of the "S" the same length and width.*

4 Make the "S" stroke again but round off the corners.

3   **4**

SIDE LOADING

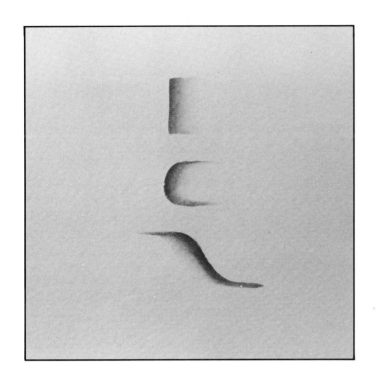

YOU WILL NEED:

#10 flat brush
one color of acrylic paint
palette
paper towels
tracing paper
small bar of soap

Side-loading is used to *shade* (using dark colors) and to *highlight* (using light colors) in tole painting.

1

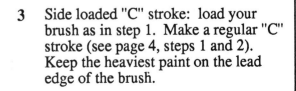

2

3

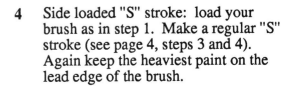

4

1 Dip your brush in <u>clean</u> water and gently blot once on each side. This will leave a small amount of water still in the brush. (With practice you'll know how much water to leave in the brush.) Pick up paint on the left corner of the brush. <u>Stay in one place on the palette</u> and stroke up and down to move the paint part way across the brush.

2 Make a stroke on your paper. Notice the paint is shaded from dark to pale.

3 Side loaded "C" stroke: load your brush as in step 1. Make a regular "C" stroke (see page 4, steps 1 and 2). Keep the heaviest paint on the lead edge of the brush.

4 Side loaded "S" stroke: load your brush as in step 1. Make a regular "S" stroke (see page 4, steps 3 and 4). Again keep the heaviest paint on the lead edge of the brush.

A PATCHWORK WELCOME

YOU WILL NEED:

one 10 1/2"x8" wooden heart
one 14"x3" wooden arch shape
acrylic paints: green sea, Salem green,
*   black green, lt. ivory*
four 3/4" long brass screw eyes
24" of 3/8" wide cream ribbon
sponge brush
#00 liner brush
sawtooth hanger
sandpaper, sealer, graphite paper,
*   palette, tracing paper, varnish (see*
*   List of Supplies, page 28)*

**A great beginning project using only
dots and lines. Patterns are on pages
7 and 26.**

1

2

3

4

1 Follow the General Directions on page 27 to prepare the boards. Use the sponge brush to paint both pieces green sea. Two coats may be necessary. Trace the patterns and transfer the lettering to the arch board. Make the dots with Salem green (see page 1). Use the liner and Salem green to paint over the letters.

2 Transfer the lines that separate the "patches" onto the heart board. Use the sponge brush and the appropriate paint to base coat each patch.

3 Use the liner and lt. ivory to make a line that covers the edges of the patches. Lt. ivory is also used to make the stitching lines around the edge of each patch and around the edge of the arch (see page 2).

4 Transfer the remaining pattern details to each patch. The details on the green sea patches are done with Salem Green. The flowers on the black green patches have sea green centers and lt. ivory petals. On the Salem green patches the lifelines (see page 2) are black green and the dots are green sea. Varnish the boards and attach the sawtooth hanger to the back of the arch. Mark where the eye screws should go and screw in place. Cut the ribbon in half and string each piece through the two screws on each side. Tie the ribbons into bows.

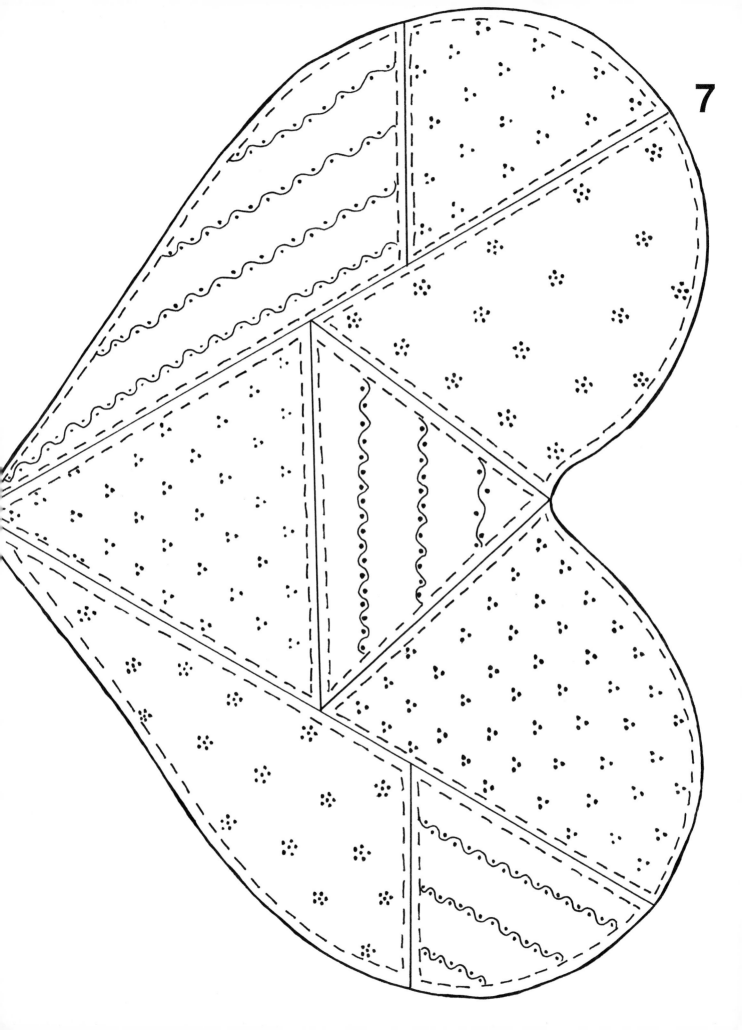

7

SHEEP ON A GATE

YOU WILL NEED:

*1 wooden sheep cut-out, this one is
   3 1/2"x3"
one 6"x4 1/2" wooden gate
acrylic paints: heritage blue, cadet
   grey, black, dusty mauve, lt. ivory
sawtooth hanger
#00 liner brush
#6 flat brush
sponge brush
paper towels
sandpaper, varnish, sealer, graphite
   paper, palette, tracing paper (see
   List of Supplies, page 28)
dried & silk baby's breath
tacky craft glue or glue gun & sticks*

**A good project for beginners. Pattern
on page 26.**

1 Follow the General Directions on page
   27 to prepare the wood pieces. With the
   sponge brush, paint the gate heritage
   blue. When dry rub the edges with
   sandpaper to achieve a weathered look.
   Paint the entire sheep cadet grey. Trace
   the sheep pattern then transfer the outline
   of the head and feet to the cut-out with
   graphite paper.

2 Crumple a paper towel and dampen
   slightly. Dip it into a nickel-size puddle
   of lt. ivory paint. Dab it on the palette
   several times then dab it lightly on the
   sheep's body and above the face to make
   the wool. Too much lt. ivory will
   prevent the grey from showing through
   (if this happens, simply dab the sheep
   with the grey paint).

3 Paint the legs, face and ears black. When
   dry, transfer the face and feet details to
   the sheep. Side load the #6 brush with
   cadet grey (see page 5) and make the
   lines to separate the legs and the hoof
   accents. Also highlight the ears and the
   sides of the head as the pattern indicates.
   Side load the #6 brush with dusty mauve
   and make the cheeks.

4 With the liner brush and grey make the
   eyes, eyelashes, eyebrows and nose. The
   eye and cheek highlights and nostrils are
   made with the liner and ivory paint. Use
   the liner and dusty mauve to paint the
   bows. Attach the sawtooth hanger to the
   back of the gate. Varnish the sheep then
   glue it to the front of the gate. Glue 2"
   sprigs of baby's breath under the sheep.

1

2

3

4

COUNTRY GOOSE WELCOME

YOU WILL NEED:

one 11 1/2" wide wooden wreath
1 geese & heart wood cut-out
three 1 1/2" wide wood hearts
acrylic paints: mendocino, cadet grey,
   golden brown, dusty mauve, brown
   iron oxide, black, white, empire
   gold
#00 liner brush
#6 flat brush
sponge brush
sandpaper, varnish, sealer, graphite
   paper, palette, tracing paper (see
   List of Supplies, page 28)
glue gun & sticks or tacky craft glue

Practice your side-loading for this project. Patterns are on pages 10 and 17.

1

2

3

4

1   Follow the General Directions on page 27 to prepare the wood pieces. With the sponge brush and mendocino paint, base coat the wreath. Base coat the geese with cadet grey and all the hearts with dusty mauve. Let dry. Sand lightly and apply a second coat if necessary.

2   Trace the geese & heart pattern and use the graphite paper to transfer it to the wood. Base coat the beak and feet with golden brown.

3   Use the #6 brush and side load (see page 5) with brown iron oxide. Paint the shadow on the beak next to the head and next to the body. Then paint the split on the beak and the division between the feet. Repeat on the second goose.

4   Mix a dime-size puddle of cadet grey with a tiny amount of black to make a darker gray. Use the #6 brush and side load it with the dark gray. Paint under the chin to shadow the neck and near the feet on the body to define the legs.

5   5 Side load the #6 brush with dusty mauve and paint the cheeks on the geese.

6   6 To make the nostrils: use the #00 liner brush and brown iron oxide and paint a basic stroke on each beak. Also use the liner and empire gold to make the basic strokes on the feet.

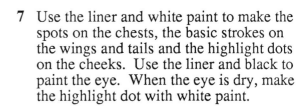

7 Use the liner and white paint to make the spots on the chests, the basic strokes on the wings and tails and the highlight dots on the cheeks. Use the liner and black to paint the eye. When the eye is dry, make the highlight dot with white paint.

7   8 Side load the #6 brush with mendocino and shade the edges of the large and small hearts. With the liner and mendocino, paint the stitches around the edges, the lettering and the design below the lettering on the big heart.

8

9 The wreath is finished with dusty mauve stitching lines around the outside and inside edges. Cadet grey is used to make the basic strokes and dots around the outside edge.

10 Varnish all the pieces. Glue the geese & heart piece on the lower part of the wreath and the three small hearts across the upper part of the wreath. Attach the sawtooth hanger to the back of the wreath.

9   **10**

LOVE MAKES LIFE BEARABLE

YOU WILL NEED:

one 7 1/2" wide wooden wreath
one 3 1/2" tall wooden teddy bear
  cut-out
two 1 1/4" wide wooden hearts
acrylic paints: dark night, bambi,
  burnt umber, napthol crimson,
  black, white, lt. ivory
sponge brush
#00 liner brush
#2 flat brush
#6 flat brush
sawtooth hanger
sandpaper, sealer, graphite paper,
  palette, tracing paper, varnish (see
  List of Supplies, page 28)
glue gun & sticks or tacky craft glue

**Side-loading is necessary for this bear.
Patterns are on page 12.**

1

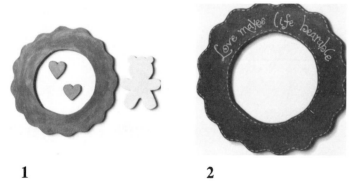

2

1 Follow the General Directions on page 27 to prepare the wood pieces. Use the sponge brush to base coat the wreath with dark night, the teddy bear with bambi and the hearts with napthol crimson. Each may require two coats. Trace all the patterns. The stitching lines on the hearts are done with the liner and dark night (see page 2).

2 Transfer all the details to the wreath. Use the liner and bambi to do stitching lines on the inside and outside front edges. The single dots are done in bambi and the triple are done in crimson (see page 1). Use the liner and bambi to trace over the letters.

3 Mark the muzzle area and the paw areas on the bear. Use the #2 brush to paint these with lt. ivory. When dry, transfer all the details to the bear.

3

4

4 Side load (see page 5) the #6 brush with burnt umber and shade the arms next to the paws and under the tummy line. Also shade around the outside of the muzzle and the inside of the ears. Side load the #6 brush with golden brown and shade the top edge of the muzzle. When dry, shade the top edge of the muzzle with crimson.

5

6

7

8

5   Use the liner and white to paint the eyes. The liner and black are used to paint the details on the paws, the pupils, the nose and the mouth. Use the liner and crimson to paint the tongue and the heart on his chest.

6   Use black on the liner to outline the muzzle, eyes and to make the eyelashes. Also use black to make the tummy line and to separate the paws from the arms with a line.

7   The stitching lines and the buttons are done in black and the eyebrows are done in burnt umber. Use white on the liner to make the highlights in the eyes and on the nose.

8   Varnish all the wood pieces. Attach the sawtooth hanger to the back of the wreath. Glue the bear to the front of the wreath at the bottom and glue a heart on each side of him.

The **"Small Goose Wreath"** on the left side is a lavender wreath with cadet grey lifelines around the edges and the basic strokes and dots are grape. There are white dots near the edge of the hat brim. The wreath on the right is green sea with deep river side edges and stitching lines. The single dots on the wreath are also deep river and the triple dots are white. White dots are painted on the edge of the hat brim and the edges of the bow.

This **"You Are Beary Special"** heart is painted dark forest. The hearts and all the stitching lines are done in bambi, while all the dots and the lettering are done in lt. ivory. The bears are bambi with brown iron oxide and lt. ivory shading.

This 13"x8" oval grapevine wreath makes a perfect place for this version of **"You Are Beary Special"**. The heart is empire gold with brown iron oxide basic stroke edging, lettering, and heart and bambi lifelines. The bears are also brown iron oxide with black and bambi used for shading. The bow is made with 2 yards of 1/2" wide green print florist ribbon.

The wreath for this **"Love Makes Life Bearable"** is painted in chrome green with burnt umber letters and stitching, napthol crimson flowers with deep river leaves. The bear is burnt umber with bambi stitching, paws and muzzle.

In this version of **"Love Makes Life Bearable"** the wreath is deep river with golden brown stitching, letters, hearts and flower centers. The petals are brown iron oxide as is the bear. His paws and muzzle are golden brown and his stitching is black.

This **"Granny Goose"** is in a 6" round, 2" deep basket with natural baby's breath behind her. The goose is cadet grey with a laguna shawl and hat. The dark shading, basic strokes, dots and ribbons are done in dark night with the light shading on the hat and shawl done in cadet grey.

This little 5 1/2" wreath does a very nice job of showing off another **"Granny Goose"**. It takes 2 3/4 yards of 1/8" wide mauve and colonial rose ribbons to wrap the wreath and make a shoestring bow with eight 2" loops and four 7" tails. Three 2", one 1 1/2" and one 3/4" wide mauve flowers are used with dried statice tucked behind them. The shawl and hat are painted gypsy rose and shaded with mendocino and white. The ribbon on the hat is white while the ribbon on the shawl is mendocino. The basic strokes on the goose and shawl are mendocino and the dots on the hat and the edge of the shawl are white.

Welcome Friends

Notice these geese feature black **"Welcome Friends"** lettering on the napthol crimson large heart. The wreath is in nightfall with white basic strokes and crimson dots near the edges. All the hearts are napthol crimson shaded with nightfall and have white basic stroke edges. The basic strokes on the geese are done in nightfall.

This **"Country Goose Welcome"** is glued to an 8"x10 1/2" wedgewood blue gate. The hearts are dark night with cape cod lettering and golden brown dotted edges. The dots and basic strokes on the geese are dark night.

This **"Love Dwells Here"** features a wreath painted in rosetta with deep river letters and stitching. The front of the heart is rosetta with deep river stitching and the side edges are burgundy rose. The boy's overalls and hat are deep river, his shirt is lt. ivory and his shoes are black. The girl's jumper and hat are burgundy rose, her blouse and pantaloons lt. ivory and her shoes are black.

The **"Love Dwells Here"** wreath shown here is dark night with cape cod stitching and lettering. The heart is cape cod with dark night lettering. The boy's overalls are cape cod, his shoes are black, his shirt is dark night and his hat is empire gold with golden brown shading. The girl's jumper is cape cod, her blouse is dark night, her pantaloons white, her shoes are black and her hat is empire gold.

This **"Patchwork Welcome"** heart is painted like the one on page 6, but instead of being tied to the arch board, it is tied to a 17"x15" vine wreath. Four stems of white dogwood, each with at least eight 2 1/2" wide blossoms, are cut into sprigs and glued to the wreath. A bow is made with 3 yards of 1/2" wide green satin ribbon and glued to the bottom of the wreath.

The lightest color used on the **"Patchwork Welcome"** shown here is palace flesh. The medium patches are rosetta and the darkest patches are coral. The lettering, stitches, dark dots and lifelines are burgundy rose. The dots near the lifelines are lt. ivory, and the ribbon ties are antique rose.

This sheep is painted like the **"Sheep On A Gate"** on page 8, but using heritage blue for the bow on the head and necklace. A heritage blue flower replaces the neck bow. The sheep is glued in a heritage blue shadow box finished with baby's breath and a puffy bow (see inside back cover).

This **"Patchwork Welcome"** uses empire gold, golden brown and brown iron oxide for the patches. The lettering is done in brown iron oxide and the stitches and the dots near the lifelines are lt. ivory. The ribbons are brown.

Welcome

YOU WILL NEED:

one 7"x5 1/2" wooden heart
two 3"x1 1/2" wooden sitting teddy
bear cut-outs
two 1" wooden hearts
acrylic paints: dark night, golden
brown, napthol crimson, empire
gold, black, white, brown iron oxide
sponge brush
#00 liner brush
#6 flat brush
sawtooth hanger
sandpaper, sealer, graphite paper,
palette, tracing paper, varnish (see
List of Supplies, page 28)
glue gun & sticks or tacky craft glue

These bears call for side-loading.
Patterns on page 19.

1 Follow the General Directions on page 27 to prepare the wood pieces. Use the sponge brush and dark night to base coat the large heart. Base coat the bears with golden brown and the hearts with napthol crimson. Two coats may be necessary on each object.

2 Trace the patterns. Transfer the details to the large heart. With a liner and golden brown make the stitching lines (see page 2). The center dots on the flowers (see page 1) are made with empire gold paint. The 5 outside dots on each flower are made with crimson.

3 Load the liner with crimson and make the lifeline around the edge of the heart (see page 2). Load the liner with empire gold paint and trace over the lettering on the heart.

4 Transfer the details to the bears. Side load (see page 5) the #6 brush with brown iron oxide and shade the ear that is behind and the inside of the front ear. Shade above the cheek, under the muzzle and under the head. Shade around the outside of the arm and above the leg that is in front. Also shade on the lower edge of the front leg and 1" up his back.

1

2

3

4

5

6

5 Side load the #6 brush with empire gold and highlight the outer part of the ear that is in front, the front edge of the muzzle and the back edge of the head. Also highlight the top of the arm and the top of the front leg.

6 Use the liner and white to paint the eye. The nose and mouth line are painted with black. Also use black to outline the eye and to paint the pupil. Pull up 5 tiny eyelashes from the pupil with the liner and black. Side load the #6 brush with napthol crimson and shade the top of the cheek. White on the liner is used to make the highlights on the cheeks, the noses and in the eyes.

7 Varnish all the pieces. When dry, attach the sawtooth hanger to the back of the heart then glue the bears facing each other near the point of the heart. Glue one small heart on each rounded part of the heart near the lettering.

7

You are beary special

YOU WILL NEED:

one 7 1/2" wooden wreath
one 2" wooden heart
1 boy and 1 girl wooden shapes, each
  2 1/2" tall
acrylic paints: cadet grey, dark night,
  napthol crimson, lt. ivory, rosetta
#00 liner brush
#2 flat brush
#6 flat brush
sponge brush
sawtooth hanger
glue gun & sticks or tacky craft glue
sandpaper, varnish, sealer, graphite
  paper, palette, tracing paper, (see
  List of Supplies, page 28)

**A bit harder project calling for
small shading. Patterns on page 21.**

2

1

1 Follow the General Directions on page
27 to prepare the wood pieces. Use the
sponge brush to base coat the wreath
with cadet grey and the heart with
napthol crimson.

2 Trace all the patterns. Transfer the
letters to the wreath and use a liner and
crimson paint to go over them. Use the
liner and dark night to make stitching
lines (see page 2) on the wreath.

3

4

3 Side load the #6 brush (see page 5) with
dark night and shade the front edge and
side of the heart. With the liner and
dark night make the stitching lines on
the heart.

4 With graphite paper, transfer the details
of the children to the wood pieces. Base
coat the girl's hat and jumper and the
boy's hat and overalls with dark night.

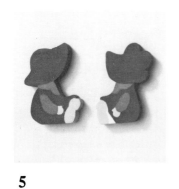

5

6

7

8

5 Use the #2 brush to base coat the sleeves, collars and shirt fronts with napthol crimson. Base coat the hands with rosetta, the shoes with cadet grey, and the girl's pantaloons with lt. ivory.

6 Side load the #6 brush with cadet grey and highlight the details on the hats. The lower edge of the jumper and the pants legs are highlighted, also the kids' backs are highlighted with cadet grey.

7 Side load the #6 brush with dark night and shade the edges of the sleeves and between the girl's feet to separate them. The edges of the shirt fronts and the boy's shoes are also shaded with dark night. The lower edge of the collars are highlighted with cadet grey.

8 Use the liner and dark night to paint the cuffs, then pull gather lines up the sleeves from the cuffs and down from the shoulder. The stitching lines are done with a liner and cadet grey and the buttons are done in dark night. Varnish all the wood pieces. Attach the sawtooth hanger to the back of the wreath and glue the heart to the lower front. The boy and girl are glued one on each side of the heart and facing each other.

Love dwells here

SMALL GOOSE WREATH

YOU WILL NEED:

one 5" wide wooden wreath
one 3" tall wooden goose cut-out
acrylic paints: napthol crimson, white
*   empire gold, burnt umber, golden*
*   brown, cadet grey, mendocino*
sponge brush
#00 liner brush
#6 flat brush
sawtooth hanger
sandpaper, varnish, sealer, graphite
*   paper, palette, tracing paper (see*
*   List of Supplies, page 28)*
glue gun & sticks or tacky craft glue

**This goose is hard because of the
tiny details. Patterns on page 23.**

1

2

3

4

1 Follow the General Directions on page 27 to prepare the wood pieces. Use the sponge brush to base coat the wreath with napthol crimson and the goose with white.

2 Use the wooden end of the liner and empire gold to make the center dots on all the flowers on the wreath (see page 1). The surrounding petals are made with mendocino. The liner and empire gold are used to make the stitching lines around the front edges of the wreath (see page 2).

3 Trace the goose pattern and transfer onto the cut-out. Base coat the hat and bow with empire gold and the beak and feet with golden brown.

4 Side load the #6 flat brush with cadet grey (see page 5) and shade the goose around the bow and near the edge of the hat. Use a liner and grey to make the stitching lines and the basic strokes (see page 3) on the goose.

5

6

7

8

5 Side load the #6 brush with burnt umber and shade under the front brim of the hat and on the brim near the ribbon. Also shade near the top edge of the hat and on the bow. Use the liner and empire gold to paint the ribbon under her chin. When dry use the liner and mendocino to paint the ribbon on the hat and the lifeline around the edge of the brim.

6 Side load the #6 brush with burnt umber and make the shading lines on the beak and feet. Use the liner and burnt umber to make the nostril on the beak.

7 Use the liner with black to make the oval eye. Side load the #6 brush with napthol crimson and make the goose's cheek. Use the liner and white to make the highlights on the cheek and eye.

8 Varnish the goose and wreath. Attach the sawtooth hanger to the back of the wreath, and glue the goose to the lower front.

GRANNY GOOSE SHADOW BOX

YOU WILL NEED:

one 4 1/2"x4 1/2" wooden goose cut-out
one 8"x6"x2 1/2" wooden box
acrylic paints: deep river, white, rosetta, cadet grey, golden brown, brown iron oxide, black, coral
2 yards of 1" wide green lacedge ribbon
#00 liner brush
#6 flat brush
sponge brush
sawtooth hanger
sandpaper, sealer, graphite paper, palette, tracing paper, varnish (see List of Supplies, page 28)
cloth covered florist wire
natural baby's breath
coral baby's breath
eleven 1" wide seafoam green silk blossoms
four to six 1" squares of cardboard
glue gun & sticks or tacky craft glue

Granny Goose calls for more detail so she is hard. Pattern on page 26.

1 Follow the General Directions on page 27 to prepare the goose. Use the sponge brush to paint the box with deep river. Two coats may be necessary. Varnish the box, attach the sawtooth hanger and set aside.

2 Use the sponge brush and white paint to base coat the goose. Trace the pattern and transfer the outline of the shawl, hat and beak to the goose. Use the #6 brush to paint the hat and shawl with rosetta and the beak with golden brown.

3 Transfer the remaining details to the goose. Use the liner brush and deep river to paint the ribbon on the hat and outline the lace scallops on the shawl. Also outline the lower edge of the shawl and make the basic strokes on the lace scallops.

4 Side load the #6 brush with cadet grey (see page 5) and shade the goose's body near the lace and her neck near the edge of the shawl. Then shade her head near the edge of the hat and under her chin. Use the liner and cadet grey to make the basic strokes on her tail (see page 3).

1

2

3

4

5

6

7

8

9

10

11

5 Side load the #6 brush with brown iron oxide and shade the lower half of the beak and next to the head. Use the liner and brown iron oxide to make the basic stroke on the beak for the nostril.

6 Side load the #6 brush with cadet grey and shade the lens areas of the glasses. Load the liner with black paint and draw a line to separate the beak from the head. When dry, outline the glasses above her beak then paint the eye. With the liner and black pull several eyelashes up from the eye.

7 Side load the #6 brush with coral and paint the shading on the hat and shawl: any part that should be the inside of a fold or crease should be shaded. Also side load with coral and shade the cheek.

8 Side load the #6 brush with white and highlight any part of the hat that should be the top part of a fold or crease. Side load the brush with cadet grey and shade the lenses of the glasses.

9 Use the liner to make the coral lines on the shawl. When dry, use the liner and deep river to make the dots on the shawl where the lines intersect. Then use the liner and white to make the dots that surround the green dots on the shawl.

10 Use the liner and white to make the highlight in the eye and on the cheek. Deep river on the liner is used to paint the bow at the neck. Varnish the goose.

11 Glue 1" squares of cardboard into the box to build the area where the goose will sit. See inside the back cover and make a bow with the ribbon and glue to the upper left corner of the box. Glue the goose to the box. Cut the dried flowers so each stem is 3" long. Dip the ends in glue and tuck under the goose. Repeat with the silks.

A Patchwork Welcome

GENERAL DIRECTIONS

BUYING YOUR WOOD: for the projects in this book use pine (a soft wood) or alder (a hard wood). Because all wood backgrounds will be painted, rather than stained, the wood grain pattern will not be noticed. Occasionally wood needs extra preparation--sand carefully and use wood putty to fill in any holes, cracks or gouges.

SANDING YOUR WOOD: it is very important that the wood be smooth before painting. Sand with a finishing grit (400 grit) sandpaper. Always sand in the same direction as the grain of the wood.

SEALING YOUR WOOD: before painting your wood it must be sealed. There are two types of sealers--water based (one that is cleaned up with soap and water) or oil based (cleaned up with paint thinner). Water based sealers that we have successfully used are Ceramcoat by Delta, Accent or JoSonja's All Purpose Sealer. Oil based sealers we like are McCloskey's Stain Controller & Wood Sealer #2931 clear or Designs From The Heart Wood Sealer. New products come on the market all the time so don't be afraid to experiment. Use a sponge brush to apply the sealer and use only one coat. If you use more than one coat of sealer, the acrylic paints will not stick. Once the sealer is dry, lightly sand with the 400 grit sandpaper or use a "wet and dry" black finishing sandpaper. It is necessary to re-sand since the sealer will raise the wood grain. Finally, wipe the wood with a tack cloth.

PAINTING YOUR WOOD BACKGROUND: since most paints come in a squeeze bottle, it is necessary to squeeze the paint onto a palette (see page 28). Use a 1" or 2" wide sponge brush to apply the paints. Be sure to keep the piece smooth, brush out any "lap" marks. When the paint is dry any paint ridges will need to be sanded. It may take two to three coats for smooth, even coverage, sand between coats of paint.

APPLYING YOUR TOLE PATTERN: see page 28 for supplies. Place the tracing paper over your chosen tole pattern and trace with a felt pen. Position the tracing paper on the wood and secure at two corners with pieces of masking tape. Be sure your painted wood background is <u>completely</u> dry or the graphite paper will not transfer. Keeping the shiny side down slide graphite paper under the tracing paper. With a stylus (or ball point pen that has run out of ink) go over the main pattern lines. Don't add the details yet. **DO NOT PRESS HARD,** or you will make permanent grooves in your wood. Remove the paper pattern and graphite paper. Now, paint your project.

FINISHING YOUR PROJECT: if there are any graphite lines showing they can be removed with a wet paint eraser or paint thinner. As the final step, all projects need to be varnished. Use a water base brushed on varnish like Ceramcoat by Delta, Accent or JoSonja's Varnish. Apply the varnish with a synthetic bristle brush since a sponge brush will cause the varnish to bubble. With any of these products use three coats (allow the varnish to dry between coats, about ten minutes each) lightly sand, wipe with a tack cloth and add a final coat.

HANGERS: a sawtooth hanger can be nailed to your finished piece.

LIST OF SUPPLIES

BRUSHES--synthetic Loew-Cornell brushes are our favorites. You'll need a small #2, medium #6 and large #10 flat plus a liner #00. For the sealer you'll need a sponge brush, and for the varnish you'll need a large synthetic brush.

BRUSH HOLDER--brushes are costly and need to be protected. It is important that the brushes be stored with the bristles up--use a clean empty food can half filled with rice, beans or sand to weight the container. Insert your brushes. Commercial brush holders are also available.

CARRY ALL--something to keep all these supplies together--a basket with a handle is nice.

CONTAINER FOR WATER--a clear glass container allows you to see when the brush is clean. Commercial containers are available or a pint canning jar is fine.

ERASER--a wet paint eraser is best; however, an art gum eraser can be used too.

GLUE--to attach painted pieces together use tacky craft glue.

GRAPHITE PAPER--this is NOT carbon paper. Graphite comes in white, black and yellow. A sheet of each color is helpful.

MASKING TAPE--to hold your tracing paper. Do not substitute cellophane tape.

PAINTS--we really like the 2 ounce squeeze bottles. See each project for a list of colors.

PALETTE--a disposable acrylic pad of special paper with a waxed surface is best. It is used to hold your puddles of paint while you work. However, you can use a sheet of glass, styrofoam meat trays or plastic plates.

PAPER TOWELS--use a good brand so the fibers do not come off on your brushes.

PEN--use a fine tip felt pen with permanent ink, any color. This kind of ink won't smear or make ridges on the original tole patterns in this book. Stitches can easily be made with this kind of pen.

RULER--a 12" ruler is useful in line work.

SANDPAPER--400 grit sandpaper or use a "wet & dry" black finishing sandpaper.

SEALER--is used to coat the wood before painting. Again a water or oil base can be used, we use both. Water based sealers include Ceramcoat Sealer by Delta, Accent Varnish & Sealer and JoSonja's All Purpose Sealer. Oil based sealers include McCloskey's Stain Controller & Wood Sealer #2931 clear or Designs From The Heart Wood Sealer.

SOAP--a small bar of hand soap to aid in cleaning brushes (see inside back cover).

STYLUS--used to transfer the pattern onto the wood and for making dots. These are available in the art supply departments. A ball point pen that has run out of ink can also be used.

TACK CLOTH--a specially treated fabric cloth that will remove any dust or particles on your project. Keep stored in a plastic bag.

TRACING PAPER--available in a pad (for smaller projects) or a roll for larger pieces.

VARNISH--is the finish coat and can be water or oil based, we prefer a water base. Ceramcoat Varnish by Delta, Accent Varnish & Sealer or JoSonja's Varnish are very good. Varnishes in spray form are also available.

WHITE CHARCOAL OR CHALK PENCIL--used directly on the project for sketching in extra details or as a guide for painting.